The Terrorist Threat to Business

Richard Latter

September 1992

WILTON PARK PAPER 62

Conference Report based on the Wilton Park Seminar on Terrorism and Business in the 1990s: Threats and Responses: 27–31 July 1992

LONDON: HMSO

© Crown copyright 1992
Applications for reproduction should be made to HMSO
First published 1992

ISBN 0 11 701725 6
ISSN 0953–8542

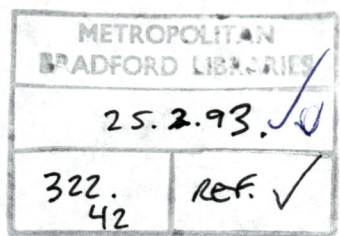

Contents

		page
1	**Introduction**	1
2	**Terrorism – Why, When and How?**	3
	State Sponsors	6
	Tactics	7
3	**Industry – Action and Reaction**	10
	The Oil Industry	11
	The Aviation Industry	12
	Shipping	15
4	**Sources of Support for Industry**	16
	The Police	17
	The Military	19
	International Organisations	21
	The Consultant	23
5	**Conclusions**	24
	List of Participants	25

1 Introduction

Terrorism involves the use of violence to bring about political change, and more particularly, to influence the political behaviour of governments. Terrorist acts "are premeditated, are intended to generate fear, and are directed at a wider target audience than the immediate victims of a particular act.... Levels of violence employed are calculated to violate society's norms and thereby maximise public outrage and consequent pressure on decision makers".[1] Terrorist groups are a threat to society in general and therefore affect the ability of industry and business to operate in that society. In addition, businesses may be targeted deliberately by terrorist groups because of their perceived links with the State, their capitalist 'credentials', and the key role they play in maintaining healthy national economies.

While governments and security forces have achieved successes against terrorism the overall effect has been containment rather than eradication. Between 1970 and 1990 an estimated 40,000 terrorist incidents occurred world wide and approximately one-third of these were against business enterprises. Following an apparent decline in numbers of international terrorist incidents in 1990, increases were recorded in 1991 and the upward trend is continuing in 1992; of the 1,301 incidents recorded in the first third of 1992, 382 attacks were directed against business. The financial costs are considerable.

While business is little concerned about theoretical definitions of terrorism, many industries have invested considerable resources and manpower to reduce possible risk. In general business has tended to react to immediate threats, or to the latest relevant incident. Its precautions have been heavily influenced by the weighing of costs of prevention versus the costs of an attack. Thus, industry's reaction has tended to be *defensive* and to emphasise the importance of cost effectiveness when taking precautions; there is an implicit and, on occasion, explicit understanding that

---

[1] Richard Latter, "Terrorism in the 1990s", *Wilton Park Paper 44*, August 1991, p. 1.

'offensive' action against terrorism is the responsibility of governments, the security forces and the courts.

However, this division of responsibility between business and government is in practice becoming less clear. The ideologically-based link made by some terrorist groups between government, business and the military has required closer co-operation between these 'targets'. Business has thus become increasingly aware of the dangers of attack, and companies' spending on 'security' has increased significantly in recent decades. This trend is likely to be reinforced in the future as victims of terrorism, either employed by companies or affected by attacks against companies, make use of their legal opportunities to seek financial redress from the companies involved; the successful law suit against Pan-Am's insurance companies in the United States is a striking recent example.

If companies are to counter potential terrorist threats effectively, a closer working relationship with relevant government agencies is essential; for example, to ensure that relevant intelligence available to either party is shared with the other. A clearer definition of responsibilities is required, if only to optimise use of available resources. While the relative cost of prevention and failure to prevent an incident will continue to affect counter-terrorist investment by business, government has wider responsibilities which make such narrow assessments of cost-effectiveness difficult. Thus, the levels of investment in defensive measures deemed to be 'necessary' by government and industry may differ. In addition, both government and industry have to decide where to invest; given governments' wider responsibilities, their efforts may be concentrated on dealing with high risk situations, crisis management and pre-emptive operations against potentially, highly-destructive groups; the collection and effective distribution of intelligence by government is clearly a priority. Should industry therefore concentrate on the 'routine', limiting its role to establishing industry-defined minimum levels of protection for assets and personnel?

Such a minimalist approach is unsuitable for certain industries, notably aviation. Given the great financial cost to the airline industry of any incident, when passengers cancel their flights after an attack for example, and the ever tougher standards being set by governments, meeting potential terrorist threats has become a key factor in the way the aviation industry conducts its business. As a result of bitter experience, Western governments, airlines and airports have co-operated increasingly, and to good effect, to deter attacks on aircraft and airports. Yet such close co-operation is by no means global even in the aviation industry and it is even less evident in other industries which are potential targets. A key issue is to decide whether government must take the leading role by forcing minimum standards on industries, for example through legislation, or whether industry itself is sufficiently aware of the terrorist problem to put its own house in order. Deciding the utility of either approach or possible alternatives is partly dependent upon a clear assessment of the nature and the extent of the terrorist threat to society and to business in particular.

2 Terrorism – Why, When and How?

If terrorism involves the threat or use of extraordinary violence for political ends, its primary purpose is to influence decision-makers in society to adopt courses of action or introduce policies which the terrorists seek. As political power is generally located in government, it is the key decision-making centre which terrorist acts are seeking to influence. Efforts to mobilise or outrage public opinion are not an end in themselves but a means to bring pressure to bear on government. Campaigns of violence may be directed against the national government of the country within which the terrorists are operating (for example, the IRA and ETA campaigns in the United Kingdom and Spain respectively), or maybe conducted at a wider international level: such international terrorism, commonly associated with Middle Eastern terrorist groups, involves terrorist campaigns conducted with the support of a foreign government or organisation and/or directed against foreign nationals, institutions, or governments. Much of the terrorism which plagued Europe in the 1970s was 'international'; even purely 'national' movements such as the Red Brigades, Red Army Faction and IRA are known to have received some support from foreign groups or countries. The role of governments in international terrorism should not be underestimated; their involvement and support has played a crucial role in the rise of modern terrorist movements and the future actions of such state-sponsors of terrorism will critically affect the levels and types of threats and risks which target governments and businesses will have to face in the 1990s.

However, the motivation of active terrorist groups is self-generated rather than imposed by sponsoring governments; motives include: left and right-wing ideology, religion, nationalism and related ethnic tensions, 'single issue' campaigns, for example for animal rights or to end the international fur trade. The relative importance of these motivations has changed in recent years. For example, the collapse of the Soviet Union and the earlier decline in importance of Maoist philosophy in China appears to have decreased the appeal of left-wing ideology and this decline, coupled with vigorous action by state security services, has undermined such groups as Action Direct, the Red Army Faction, and the Red Brigades[2]. In contrast an increase of right-wing violence has occurred in Europe in 1992, notably in Germany and France, which may yet spawn a new generation of right-wing terrorist groups.

The break-up of the former Soviet Union and the resulting end of the Cold War have generated an upsurge of nationalism in Eastern Europe and Central Asia, which has already resulted in wars in former Yugoslavia, Moldova, Georgia, Armenia and Azerbaijan. It is highly likely that the resolution of such conflicts will leave disgruntled 'losers' who will be prepared to use terrorist tactics

---

[2] It should be noted, however, that the RAF, for example, remains active despite the loss of Stazi support from the former GDR. Also, the Dev Sol and Shining Path Groups in Turkey and Peru respectively, remain active.

given the hatreds which these ethno-nationalist conflicts are generating. In almost all cases, the opposing factions in these wars are represented by significant minorities in many other European states; the possibility that these groups will re-enact far away hostilities on the streets of their host nations can not be discounted.

However, this threat remains as yet potential and in the short term nationalist-motivated terrorist activity in Europe appears likely to be reduced as the Palestinian groups curtail their activities as the Middle East peace process proceeds, or they are restrained by their state sponsors for the same reason. The rise and fall of variously-motivated groups has implications for business in particular; for example, while left-wing movements have explicitly targeted 'the military-industrial complex' and animal rights groups direct attacks against particular companies, nationalist terrorism may be less intensively focused on business activity. Nevertheless, campaigns to undermine targeted economies have been organised, for example by the IRA in Northern Ireland, and similar campaigns to undermine regional or national economies may yet emerge, for example, in the new states created from Yugoslavia and the former Soviet Union.

It is unclear whether changes in the motivation of active terrorist movements will continue; for example, increasing right-wing violence in Europe may yet generate a left-wing response, including the use of terrorist tactics. Yet, whatever the outcome, it *is* clear that highly motivated and adequately financed terrorist groups will continue to operate effectively. While the very nature of their activity enables them to achieve some 'success' without recourse to sophisticated technology and planning, there is little doubt that groups have been particularly effective when backed by state sponsors who have been able to back high motivation and ruthlessness with effective training and equipment. For example, the support by the East German Stazi for the RAF enabled the group to conduct increasingly sophisticated acts and the support for the Palestinian cause by, for example, Iraq, Iran and Syria, similarly extended the reach of Palestinian terrorist groups and enabled them to conduct increasingly complex operations.

State Sponsors

The linkage between state sponsors and terrorist groups exists because of perceived mutual benefits. Terrorist groups allow themselves to be used by state sponsors if there is a compatability of aim and if the state is able to furnish resources required by the group: high technology weapons systems and explosives, intelligence resources for planning and reconnaissance, funding safe houses, base support, medical aid and immunity from retaliation, use of the diplomatic bag for movement of supplies, passports and identification papers. States use terrorist groups to pursue foreign policy goals which cannot be pursued openly or which may not be achievable by direct state action. The use of such groups enables a state to plausibly deny its involvement in an event particularly if the operation fails. Every effort is made to ensure that the link between the state and the group is as distant and concealed as possible. However, too tenuous a link and a high level of group independence means that state control of operations may be limited; for this reason the state's own operatives may be drawn into operations (the Lockerbie incident and Libyan involvement is an example).

From the point of view of the target state or business, state sponsorship means that their terrorist opponents are better organised, equipped and more mobile, and therefore pose a greater risk. If the current resurgence in nationalism continues and, indeed, the successful meeting of nationalist aspirations by groups breaking away from the former Soviet Union occurs, this may increase the number of states involved with terrorist groups; as new states emerge they may be encouraged to support their 'fellow countrymen' rebelling in neighbouring states. The successful secessions of, for example, the Baltic States, Croatia and Slovenia can only serve to encourage similarly motivated groups outside Europe, for example, the Sikhs in the Punjab, the Tamils in Sri Lanka, the people of East Timor, the Muslims in the southern Philippines; that is, the dissatisfied and disaffected in all multi-ethnic states. If such an increase in nationalist-related terrorism is anticipated, businesses, particularly those engaged in multinational enterprise, need to assess even more carefully the likely methods and tactics to be used by new terrorist groups and the level of risk they pose.

Tactics

Close links between a state sponsor and terrorist group can affect how the group behaves, for example how it selects its targets. Thus, the relative infrequency of attacks against the oil industry by Middle Eastern groups reflects the benefits which state sponsors such as Iraq and Iran derive from their role as oil exporters. More generally, a rapprochement between sponsoring states and their political adversaries may lead to a cessation or redirection of terrorist activity; the Syrian rapprochement with the West resulting from the Gulf War is an example.

Civilians remain the main target of terrorist activity: between 40 and 49 per cent of all attacks were targeted against the general public in 1990 and 1991 respectively. Attacks against political and diplomatic targets accounted for 26 and 16 per cent respectively in 1990 and 1991, while the military and police were attacked in 21 per cent of cases in both years. In Africa, the Americas and the Middle East political and diplomatic targets suffered more than police and military while the reverse is seen in Europe. According to these estimates, business facilities and personnel accounted for only 8 per cent of targets, although, of course, the disruption caused by terrorism in general also affected business. It should also be noted that other sources (see page 1) give a higher incidence of 'business related' incidents. These differences reflect different approaches to gathering data and in defining what constitutes a terrorist act. Whatever the definition the problem remains important.

Bombing remains the most common terrorist tactic because it is the simplest and least risky method of attack; 41 per cent of total incidents in 1991 involved bombings. The three most common tactics involved bombing, shootings and ambush raids; together these constituted 90 per cent of all incidents in 1990 and 86 per cent of all incidents in 1991. Kidnapping, hostage-taking and hijacking and sabotage were far less commonly used, constituting

10 per cent and 15 per cent of total incidents in 1990 and 1991 respectively. There were only 52 recorded kidnappings in 1990, mostly in Latin America, and 132 recorded kidnappings in 1991, mainly in Latin America and Europe: most of these incidents involved criminals or organised crime.

An important development in the second half of the 1980s involved increased links between terrorism and drugs trafficking; however, politically motivated terrorist groups appear to be involved in the trade to secure funding for their activities rather than adopting the dissemination of drugs as a long term strategy to achieve a political goal. Criminal drug cartels, particularly in Colombia, have adopted terrorist tactics to seek to minimise government action against their activities, but they do not appear to be seeking a broader political change.

There is some evidence that the targeting and overall tactical approach of terrorist groups differs with their motivation. For example, the left-wing philosophy of the Red Army Faction involved it in a deliberate effort to seek the support of left-wing political groupings in Germany. As a result, the RAF sought to limit the numbers of civilian casualties and explicitly targeted the 'military-industrial complex' in Europe. Attacks were directed against establishment leaders and these included people from and associated with the business community. In contrast, nationalist and right-wing terrorist groups appear to be less discriminating and therefore are more prepared to target the general public and 'establishment' figures in relatively junior positions. However, such differences of approach are by no means clear cut and change over time; for example, there is evidence that the RAF is broadening its 'campaign' to include medium level civil servants who are involved in government programmes which they (the RAF) deem to be socially exploitative.

Excluding the ideologically-motivated, most attacks against business are undertaken to: drive out investment and thereby undermine the targeted economy, to secure payment of protection money to fund terrorist activities, to disrupt society in general. For some single issue terrorist groups, however, attacks on business form the key component to their strategy: for example, those seeking to end the fur trade, those seeking to diminish or end meat consumption, those engaged in product contamination.

Attacks against specific products are generally motivated by a grudge against the companies, or political aims, or criminal extortion. Grudge attacks are the most dangerous because the aim is to maximise damage. Attacks can therefore be made without warning and are designed to kill; it should be noted that the grudge element may develop in erstwhile politically-motivated groups: massacres at airports and mid-air aircraft bombings appear to have been motivated in part by a desire for revenge. However, in general political attacks against products are less dangerous because the aim is to secure publicity and deaths are perceived to be counter-productive (eg by the animal rights movement). Similarly, criminal attacks are less dangerous because those involve seeking financial reward; contamination is therefore unlikely or contaminated samples will be guarded (by the extortionist) against purchase because if they are eaten extortion will no longer be possible. For companies seeking to deal with such attacks it is vital that the motives of the terrorists are clearly established in order to assess how best to respond. Attacks designed to kill will require immediate withdrawal of a product whereas 'extortion' may enable a more flexible response to be adopted with a view to apprehending the criminals involved.

In making such judgements, however, business must work closely with the police and relevant government agencies. For this to be done effectively adequately co-operation must be developed before incidents occur. Anticipation of problems is a key element in developing an adequate business response to terrorism. Decisions on whether to invest, the levels of investment to be made, protection of facilities and personnel to be developed and how to deal with incidents all require 'pre-emptive' investment of companies' resources. This has been recognised by most of the major multinational corporations, particularly in the oil, aviation and shipping industries.

3   Industry – Action and Reaction

It is a truism that in an increasingly interdependent international economy business activity is increasingly international; it not only involves large multinational corporations but also smaller companies operating in regional international markets. When companies consider expanding into foreign markets their decisions are dominated by business considerations and assessments of risk of terrorism are set within this wider context. The approach appears to be to assess the level of risk and then to consider how best to manage risk to minimise disruption of company activities; it is rare for the economic factors favouring expansion to be overridden by perceived risk of terrorist attack. The aim is to marshal resources to ensure that the company is well-informed about the local situation and takes adequate precautions to protect personnel, installations, and business activity.

Any company must take the following steps when entering a new country. Close contacts must be established with diplomats and embassies in the relevant country. They will be well-informed about existing economic conditions, the activities of local terrorist groups, their modes of operation, the nature and effectiveness of government response, levels of popular support for the police, the efficiency of local intelligence organisations. Most importantly, they will have a clear idea of who can be trusted in the country to give accurate and honest information. Effective company links with representatives of their own governments are essential. In addition, major companies with sufficient financial resources may establish their own teams to assess local risks, calculate costs of potential damage and establish the means by which these can be minimised. However, such groups can not work on their own; they need to link effectively with local police and security agencies. The company must establish an effective crisis management committee, linked to such agencies, whose task is to focus completely on any crisis to the exclusion of all other factors. The existence of such a group enables the rest of the company to continue with its principal job, that of trading and conducting commercial business. Training of staff, increasing security at potential target facilities and other precautionary measures should be organised by this specialist group.

In areas of political instability companies may strengthen support for their presence within the local community by developing social, educational and sporting programmes, for example. These have achieved successes, where properly managed and subjected to proper financial controls. However, such programmes may also generate conflict and terrorist attacks if local communities are already deeply divided and not sufficiently protected by national police and security agencies; attacks by Sandero Luminoso in Lima against supporters of company-sponsored projects demonstrate such difficulties.

These general approaches to be taken by companies operating in foreign countries do not adequately reflect the need to design specific response strategies for particular industries. The problems experienced by, for example, the oil, aviation, and shipping industries reflect important differences and industry-specific problems which have dominated company counter-terrorism measures.

The Oil Industry

As terrorism increased in the 1970s the oil industry appeared to be a likely target. It produced vulnerable and highly inflammable products which, if ignited, would provide spectacular publicity for the terrorist group involved. Many companies operated in areas of political instability, for example in the Middle East, where access to potential targets appeared to be relatively easy. In addition, they were symbolic targets representing Western capitalism and wealth. As such they were also natural targets for extortion.

In practice the number of attacks against the industry has been relatively limited; since the Japanese Red Army attack against a refinery in Singapore in 1975 the number of incidents has been relatively small and is declining. Examples include the targeting of BP by the IRA as the supplier of oil products to the RUC and British Army, but even here the campaign of attacks against service stations and related targets appears to have ceased since 1981. More recently the Gulf War prompted a number of attacks against oil industry installations in the Gulf region by Iraqi sympathisers but the level and success of attacks was far below predictions, largely due to Western diplomatic approaches and warnings to potential state sponsors. Attacks against pipelines average six a year, but the overall trend for the highly capable terrorist groups appears to have been away from industrial targets towards assassination and attacks against people. The greatest risk to the oil industry is the general threat terrorism poses to society.

Nevertheless, oil companies have been particularly active in building close relations with governments and security agencies in the countries where they operate. They have worked assiduously to ensure access to reliable travel and threat assessments. They issue detailed guidelines on personnel and asset protection and seek to enhance standards of protection where the threat is deemed to be particularly severe. Thorough contingency planning has been undertaken to ensure that companies can meet crisis situations adequately. In Third World countries building good community relations plays an important role. While protection of assets by security personnel is undertaken, companies have not sought to usurp the primary role of local government forces for policing and armed security; a clear distinction is made between the essentially defensive arrangements which may legitimately be made by the company and the intelligence-gathering, policing and the actions of the security forces which are the responsibility of government.

The Aviation Industry

The distinction between government and industry roles is perhaps less clear in aviation. The accessibility of airports, the large numbers of people passing through, their glamour and their important role as a gateway for business and international travellers makes them an ideal target for terrorist groups seeking publicity and to disrupt local economies. The history of regular and at times frequent attacks over the last 25 years has resulted in particularly close government-industry relationships in many countries.

The threats to aviation include hijacking, armed attack against airports, bombing of aircraft in the air, the use of car bombs in or near an airport, making bomb threats to close down an airport. The effects of terrorism on the aviation industry include deaths of and injury to employees and customers, the loss of business to airlines, an increase in public fear of flying, the costs and inconvenience of greater airport security and the reduction of its aim to be user friendly. More recently the successes of victims and relatives of victims in securing legal redress and financial compensation for the 'failure' of the industry to protect customers has provided a further incentive to continue the already major improvements in security which have been achieved in most, if not all, countries.

Counter-measures are designed to meet the peculiar problems associated with a mass transportation industry. These include for example: access control to the airport (dividing into landside and airside areas), the introduction of computerised ID cards, a 20 year background check on staff, the screening of all staff as they move airside, screening of all passengers and hand luggage, screening of all transfer luggage, selectively screening hold baggage. These types of measures are a mixture of technological and organisational approaches. The introduction of new technologies to screen baggage, for example Thermal Neutron Analysis, X-ray and vapour sniffer technology, and their use in combination to help to offset each system's weaknesses is a promising development. Yet, the problem remains of how to make such technology available worldwide.

Similarly, improvements in staff training and motivation in some airports, the use of passenger profiling to improve screening procedures and efforts to segregate departing and arriving passengers improve security at specific airports, but a lack of uniformity of standards worldwide will ensure that opportunities for air terrorism will remain considerable. The research of airlines and aircraft builders into the possibilities for strengthening baggage containers in airframes and the introduction of weakened panels to limit the effect of blast to an airborne aircraft, if and when they are introduced to carrier fleets, would represent a significant step forward.

As with the oil industry effective co-operation with local police, specialised units of the military, national security services and foreign aviation authorities is essential if the central aim of *deterring* attacks is to be achieved.

With the undoubted improvement in security in many of the world's airports the key problem is how to ensure adequate and common levels of security throughout the aviation industry. It is well-known that security arrangements are weak at some airports and it is known that these 'loopholes' in the system are exploited by terrorists. It is unclear how the aviation industry and relevant inter-governmental agencies can enforce common international standards. The International Civil Aviation Organisation lacks both the brief and resources to play such a role. A possible way forward is for governments with high national security standards and the airlines which use airport facilities to press others for similar improvements.

The potential reduction in numbers of passengers travelling to, and hence business occurring within a given airport is a potent threat. If discreet warnings to an airport that security is lax do not bring about an adequate response, public warnings are entirely justified. For example, it is estimated that the public criticism of security arrangements at Athens Airport in the mid-1980s cost the airport $300 million in lost revenues. If all else fails airlines should boycott the airport concerned and, indeed, interested governments can play a role by, for example, forbidding in-bound flights from the country where the security problem exists. In addition, financial help may need to be given to poorer countries to pay for the introduction of modern technology, and to monitor its efficacy; delays in achieving 'globalised' standards should not undermine efforts to introduce rigorous security arrangements, for example, within the OECD countries.

Shipping

Terrorist attacks against shipping have been mercifully rare, the 'Achille Lauro' and 'City of Poros' incidents in the 1980s being exceptional. However, criminal activity against the shipping business is widespread and criminals' successes demonstrate the potential vulnerability of the industry to terrorism. Criminal activity mainly involves piracy and/or fraud.

Modern piracy is concentrated in Far Eastern waters and the seas off West Africa, although incidents are not unknown elsewhere, for example in the Mediterranean. Attacks fall into three broad categories: short-term seizure of a ship in order to rob the crew or to steal parts of a cargo, longer term seizures enabling the whole cargo to be stolen and off-loaded, permanent seizure of the ship for resale or use by the group involved in the hijack. Cases of fraud are regularly reported which involve losses of fictional cargoes leading to insurance claims, or the sale of non-existent cargoes. Both piracy and fraud are increasingly well-run by organised criminal gangs. There is evidence that these groups are also involved in drug trafficking.

The central problem for law enforcement agencies dealing with shipping crime is the difficulty of establishing clear jurisdiction in a given case. Often as many as ten countries are involved (eg the countries where the ship is registered, where the crime occurred, where the stolen goods were off-loaded and sold, where the organisers of a crime are located). As a result, both government and industry have failed to respond effectively. In addition, the nature of the international shipping industry further complicates law enforcement. The use of flags of convenience is widely abused, for example some countries having no clear record of how many ships are registered under their flag.

Concern has been relatively low key as theft is not regarded in some quarters as a 'social' crime. It is noticeable for example that efforts to take strong action occurred in the seas around Vietnam because of reports of atrocities against the Boat People rather than because of seizures of goods. In addition, many countries are loath to pursue cases because they are extremely expensive to investigate and many countries lack experience and trained manpower to prosecute enquiries effectively. There is little doubt that many of these problems would arise in the event of serious terrorist incidents occurring.

While the shipping industry has been slow to react, countermeasures have been introduced and others are under consideration. Some ships and companies have made efforts to 'harden the target' by improving the training of ships crews, by issuing arms to crew members, and by improving the overall security of vessels, whether in port or at sea. The more widespread deployment of naval forces under UN auspices has been suggested, to take place in the regions where piracy is particularly acute. An additional idea is to run escorted convoys through areas where piracy is common. Yet, it remains far from clear whether the industry is sufficiently concerned, or that such concern extends broadly enough through the industry to meet the problem effectively; various technological aids, including, for example, the introduction of satellite tracking equipment have not been taken up. The maritime industry remains a 'closed' society and it is difficult to get it to enforce common standards of behaviour. There appears to be a strong case for greater action by governments and related agencies to take the lead. This would require effective international collaboration between the governments concerned and their security forces.

4 Sources of Support for Industry

Co-operation of government and government agencies with business is designed to achieve 'relative' security, namely, to introduce the achievable rather than 100 per cent blanket security. Assessments differ regarding what is 'achievable', the appropriateness of a given level of expenditure and the division of costs between public and private sectors. In the West, governments' recent greater emphasis on market forces implied an increased role for industry in maintaining its own security. In addition, the progressive strengthening of health and safety legislation required the introduction of better safety technology and training which, although directed primarily against the risk of accident, nevertheless improved overall resilience to potential terrorist attacks. Finally, rising insurance premiums and their linkage with the adequacy of companies' pre-emptive measures further strengthened their resolve to improve security. However, the essential division of labour existing between government agencies, represented in the first instance by the police, and industry remains unchanged.

The Police

What are the respective roles of the police and companies during a terrorist incident? While it is essential that responsibilities for pre-emption and prevention be shared, government's role is paramount in for example: gathering intelligence, its analysis, decisions on information sharing, deployment of security and police forces. Yet business can still contribute significantly, for example, through the proper vetting of employees, the adequate selection and training of security personnel and by meeting the cost of security provisions, by employing specialist consultants. At the reaction and investigation stages of an incident the police have the leading role, but business reactions can also be important. The availability of adequate fire-fighting, first-aid, and crisis reaction teams, all supported by adequate training, can contribute to limiting the damage caused by a terrorist incident.

Clearly, company responsibilities do not extend to public space, which is the routine responsibility of the police as part of their normal order maintenance role. However, in the 'private space' of company facilities, regular police involvement will be minimal and companies may opt for totally private security arrangements. In this situation the quality of cover provided, levels of training of personnel, adequate experience in the security field and proper equipment are vital. To be effective staff have to be well-paid and motivated and suitable technology provided. In such instances the case for seeking advice from and liaising with the police remains strong. For example, the Euro-Tunnel company responsible for the English terminal of the UK-France Channel Tunnel employs its own security staff to ensure the physical security of the terminal (the French terminal will be policed by the French police). Company-police co-operation is high; liaison channels have been established, the police will help to train the security staff and ensure close co-operation with the private security regime established by Euro-Tunnel. This kind of close linkage could be extended to many other industrial facilities.

The advantages of close co-operation are increasingly recognised by companies and police forces alike. Problems remain however. The sharing of information on a 'need-to-know' basis and reluctance to disseminate widely sensitive information permeates most state agencies and police forces. This continues to limit effective information sharing. The generally positive government-company relationships established in the OECD countries are not mirrored elsewhere. For example, businesses in the former Soviet Union may be reluctant to co-operate with the vestiges of a state security system which is steeped in anti-entrepreneurial/capitalist ideology and practice. Furthermore, the undermining of government authority, the crisis in Russian public finance, and the breakdown of morale in the security services all contribute to poor organisation and a lack of modern policing equipment. In these circumstances state police forces are often unable to provide the support which local businesses, whether privatised or still under state control, require. In this situation well-equipped and organised 'private' security companies are being established to provide security. Unfortunately, in the current chaotic situation the borderline between legitimate security provision and protection racketeering is not always well-defined.

Elsewhere both Western and local companies are confronted with decisions on how best to conduct their business in states where the authorities are using the police and security forces to terrorise their own populations. Historically companies have been prepared to continue trading in such states and have worked with local security forces to ensure protection for company assets and personnel. This approach has been criticised, not least on moral grounds. Nevertheless, withdrawing from a particular country and its market is a costly and difficult decision; the adage that 'business is business and politics should be left to the politicians' appears to be the norm. Companies are only likely to withdraw or cease trading with a state sponsor of terrorism or with a repressive regime when forced to do so by home government legislation. Even embargoes, whether nationally or internationally imposed, are widely flouted by companies seeking to promote their own business interests. Supplying the chemical and biological weapons industries of Iraq and Syria are two notable and notorious recent examples. Such illegal trade has resulted in the prosecution and imprisonment of the company directors involved, which hardly benefits company-police co-operation.

Some argue that close co-operation to facilitate the security of company assets is inevitably undermined if companies trade with regimes which are sponsoring the very terrorist threat which both companies and governments seek to resist. Unfortunately, the record of some companies has been less than adequate in this respect. Clearly, effective government, police and company co-operation is essential to avoid frictions and prosecutions. The government-company relationship is symbiotic; each requires a clear understanding of the other's policies and goals and has to adjust their own on occasion for mutual benefit. In extreme cases governments may resort to the use of military force to resolve a situation, either when dealing with a state-sponsored terrorist incident or *in extremis* when dealing with the state-sponsoring regime itself. Such action may critically affect business operations.

The Military

Countering terrorism involves dissuasion or deterrence in the first instance, the minimisation of the effects of an attack if deterrence fails, and punishment of the perpetrators, where possible, through retaliation. The military can be involved at all stages, for example in information gathering, physical protection of people and property, defusing bombs, patrolling troubled districts. However, it also fulfils a unique 'offensive' role through its capability to use armed force against terrorists. Notwithstanding the successes of policing and the use of the courts, exercising the military option is a consistent feature of policy for governments faced with terrorism. The threat of the use of military force and the use of such force have been used publicly and covertly to deter attack, and destroy terrorist groups. Some countries have established specialist military units; the United States for example has strengthened its 'Special Operation Forces' and provided them with appropriate material and training for an anti-terrorist mission. These forces are an integral part of the US counter-terrorist strategy. Other countries have developed similar units, although the legal guidelines governing their use vary considerably; for example, in Sweden the military may only deal with external security threats whereas French forces may be called into action in France where police forces appear to be out-matched.

For the threat of force to be credible, actions actually undertaken must be seen to be successful. Failures serve only to reinforce terrorism, encouraging the terrorists, and undermining public support for and confidence in the government and law enforcement agencies. Even successful operations, if publicised, are not uniformly well-received; Israeli operations in Lebanon, the American air-raid on Libya, and UK military operations against the IRA in Gibraltar have all prompted considerable public disquiet, both domestically and abroad. Support for the use of the military option varies according to differing perceptions of terrorism: whether it is essentially a criminal act, or an act of warfare. If terrorism is 'a crime' it is for the police and legal institutions of a state to secure its abatement and destruction; the implication is that the military has a role to play only in exceptional circumstances. Actions must be governed by due respect for law and the norms of a democratic society. For those who view terrorism as 'war', a more robust reaction is countenanced and the use of military sanctions is an appropriate response to be used at need. This debate extends into the international field where countries threatened by state-sponsored terrorist groups have at times opted for diplomatic persuasion and, at worst, have bowed to terrorist demands (eg in hostage situations), while others have responded with military force.

Recourse to the military option against state-sponsors poses particular problems for businesses; companies operating in the states attacked are vulnerable to retribution if they are associated with the country undertaking military action. It is for this reason that many multinational corporations seek to distance themselves from the activities of their home governments. For example, US and UK oil interests continued to operate in Libya after the Tripoli bombings of 1986.

International Organisations

The use of military force to counter terrorism remains in general an option of last resort. Such operations are usually unilateral or involve only a few states. In contrast policing efforts to counter terrorism have become increasingly multinational in the past two decades, with organisations such as INTERPOL, the Trevi Group, and the Schengen Group being actively involved in co-ordinating national anti-terrorist policies.

Many argue that INTERPOL as the foremost international police organisation should play a key role in the exchange of police and criminal information at bilateral, regional and international levels. Indeed, in 1986 INTERPOL received such a mandate from its 158 member countries and a guide for combatting international terrorism was disseminated to all member states. The guide outlines the type of information, the procedures for co-operation and exchange of information, the system for alerts and warnings, and the services offered by the General Secretariat in Lyon. INTERPOL has established liaison arrangements with the International Civil Aviation Organisation, International Air Transport Association and the Airports Association Council International. The aim is to establish effective liaison and information sharing and the organisation has achieved recent successes; for example, it received and exchanged information concerning the bombing of the Israeli Embassy in Buenos Aires, on activities of individuals allegedly belonging to an anti-Turkish criminal group, as well as on individuals associated with ETA criminal activities in Spain.

Such initiatives receive considerable support: it is a widely held view that developing stronger information sharing and security co-operation not only increases states' security, but also that of the business community. Stronger ties and co-operation between business, the private sector, not only with their own governments but also with appropriate international organisations can only be beneficial. Many accept that the business community, through its own networks, can play a valuable role in some countries, not least by liaising with local police effectively.

The increasing development of institutionalised co-operation is essential because it enables individual contacts to be formalised to ensure that they continue over time as personnel change. It is intended to break down barriers between organisations, build contacts and share information. However, the problem of information-sharing remains particularly difficult; organisations remain reluctant to share information with outside agencies. Some argue, for example, that INTERPOL is not secure and not useful for information exchange on terrorism. The membership of known state-sponsors reinforces this perception. It is also unclear which organisation should organise a co-ordinated data base. INTERPOL, Trevi, Schengen, and various national police forces all appear to be committed to establishing their own data bases. The problems of linkage and co-ordination are evident.

Some suggest that these problems be met by the creation of a European Police Force which will be empowered to investigate particular types of crime, including terrorism, on a European-wide scale. However, there are formidable difficulties, not least the problem of reconciling differing legal systems, even among the European Community member states, for example. It is also far from clear that the political will exists in European governments for the project to be viewed as realistic. The recent problems with ratification of the Maastricht Treaty have undoubtedly set the process back.

Despite such problems, much is being done. National police forces in Europe do co-operate effectively via Trevi and the Schengen system. Bilateral contacts are increasing and the positive contacts being established with the newly independent states of Eastern Europe represent a considerable step forward. Their active participation in European counter-terrorism efforts is a double bonus; their information-gathering and sharing brings results and their recent sponsorship of terrorist groups has been curtailed.

The need is to ensure that international organisations avoid competition and duplication of effort. However, this is a process which can only be set in hand by government. The influence of business remains marginal although the results of better international integration of the counter-terrorism effort certainly would be beneficial to it.

The Consultant

There is little doubt that the failure of the international community to suppress effectively terrorist movements has prompted business to take steps independently to maintain company security. While such work may be undertaken in co-operation with government agencies, companies do act with a considerable-degree of independence. Many companies employ security consultants to help them assess threats or risks and to offer expertise on how best to minimise dangers to company personnel, installations and business.

What services can the consultant offer and what advantages does he bring over and above the support received from government agencies? His or her threat assessment does not involve predictions. The intention is to advise the company on how it may best be received positively in a country where it wishes to operate. While embassies are useful and to be consulted, their purpose is to promote government rather than business policy; the two need not coincide. In addition, embassies are part of the host country's 'establishment' society and are therefore unlikely to have contacts with rebel factions. Companies need to be well-informed about such groups and consultants are able to establish contacts. The overall aim of threat assessments is to set a base-line against which security policy can be drawn up, to develop a security programme and determine the likelihood of a company receiving due payment for its effort in a given economy. The analyst has to be as professional and as objective as possible. He or she has to inform the client about local conditions before the company enters into a new area and ensure that it is not taken unawares by political change or the sudden fulfilment of 'worst case' scenarios.

Key factors involved in analysts' threat assessments include: distinguishing a regime's core sources of support, and analysing the elements and strengths of political opposition; examining social and economic trends supporting or undermining ruling and opposition groups; considering potential internal and external threats; providing indicators on what would have to happen for change to occur and assessing the probability of such change. Finally, the impact of change on a corporation's business is assessed.

Companies employ consultants to undertake political risk analysis because these experts have the time and expertise to undertake the job, which companies lack. They are usually more cost-effective than setting up an in-house operation and external analysts can provide follow-up research if required. The overall intention of the analyst is not to discourage companies operating in a given country but to encourage them to do so in a safe way.

5 Conclusions

The threat of international terrorism remains considerable; rising nationalism in Europe, in particular, may lead to an increase in incidents. Both governments and businesses must, consequently, remain wary and continue to invest substantially in their efforts to counter terrorism. Close co-operation is essential but a clear division of responsibilities and of tasks is also needed. Governments meet terrorism with a combination of offensive and defensive measures in the 'public space' while industry's role must remain defensive and confined to protecting its private space (installations) and personnel. Industry does not and should not seek to usurp or replace the security responsibilities of the state. However, effective industry involvement does enable the state to reduce related funding for physical security, and use it elsewhere, and also to manage better the overall situation.

Nevertheless, industry has the right to expect government to take the lead by, for example, framing and enforcing adequate legislation, maintaining adequate security services, sharing information with industry as required. Government failures may result in 'inappropriate' trading patterns and sales (eg to state sponsors of terrorism), the evolution of ill-organised and indisciplined private security agencies (eg in the former Soviet Union) and the requirement by industry to invest more heavily in security activity, which diverts companies from their primary objective, conducting business.

While company security standards and levels of government-business co-operation have increased significantly in the OECD countries, standards elsewhere are lower and even declining. This division has to be removed for international terrorism exploits the 'weakest links'. Western governments, security agencies and companies need to begin to extend their horizons further. How best to transfer positive experience and counter terrorism know-how to the new democracies of East Europe, for example, represents an enormous new challenge which government and business alike will have to face.

List of Participants

ABBOTT, Paul: British Rail HQ, London
ABHYANKAR, Jayant: ICC International Maritime Bureau, London
ALEXANDER, Yonah: Elliott School of International Affairs, The George Washington University, Washington DC
ATAÖV, Turkkaya: Ankara University
BAER, Alain: Ecole Polytechnique CREST, Paris
BELL, Alexander: Shell International Petroleum Company, London
BROTHERS, George: Digital Equipment Co Ltd, Fareham
BURDIS, Michael: South Yorkshire Police, Sheffield

CLARK, Stewart: Tayside Police, Dundee
CLUTTERBUCK, Richard: University of Exeter
DENTON, Geoffrey: Wilton Park
EDWARDS, Stanley: Ministry of Defence Police, London
GIBSON, Peter: Strathclyde Police, Glasgow
GIFFARD, John: North Yorkshire Police
GOUGH, Terry: British Petroleum plc, London
GREGORY, Frank: University of Southampton
HAEBERER, Peter-Michael: Berlin Police Force
HELLENTHAL, Markus: Border Police and Immigration, Ministry of the Interior, Bonn
HORCHEM, Hans Josef: Institut Terrorismus Forschung, Bonn
HOWLEY, John: Metropolitan Police, London
IRWIN, John: Dartmouth Publishing Company Ltd, Aldershot
JANKE, Peter: Control Risks Information Services Ltd, London
KROHNE, Steve: Marion Merrell Dow Inc, Kansas City
LATTER, Richard: Wilton Park
LAVEY, Donald: INTERPOL, Lyon
McGREGOR, Ian: British Transport Police, London
MORITZ, Lothar: German Committee of European Security and Co-operation
MORRIS, Eric: Strategic and Security Consultant, Cardiff
NIANIOS, Nicolaos: Security Directorate of Attika, Athens
OLANDER, Jan: Ministry of Foreign Affairs, Stockholm
PEARSON, Michael: Gatwick Airport, Sussex
RAMM, Roy: New Scotland Yard, London
SCHMIDT-RANTSCH, Jürgen: Federal Ministry of Justice, Bonn
VAN CLEAVE, Steve: Inter-American Consultants, Marietta, Georgia
VERPOORTEN, Edgard: Joint Anti-Terrorist Group, Brussels
WHINNETT, Ian: Hertfordshire Constabulary
WIESE, Walter: Permanent Delegation of Germany to NATO, Brussels
WORRALL, Terence: British Rail, London

Printed in the United Kingdom for HMSO
Dd 294583 11/92 C6 3397/7 10170